PIANO • VOCAL SELECTIONS

WHITE CHRISTMAS
THE MUSICAL

MUSIC AND LYRICS BY IRVING BERLIN

ISBN 978-1-4234-6350-4

Cover art courtesy of SpotCo

Irving Berlin Music Company®
www.irvingberlin.com

EXCLUSIVELY DISTRIBUTED BY

HAL•LEONARD®
CORPORATION
7777 W. BLUEMOUND RD. P.O. BOX 13819 MILWAUKEE, WI 53213

Visit Hal Leonard Online at
www.halleonard.com

DREAMING OF "IRVING BERLIN'S WHITE CHRISTMAS"

BY TED CHAPIN

This songbook reflects the songs from the stage musical "Irving Berlin's *White Christmas.*" Yes, the stage musical is based on the famous Paramount movie with the same name, but this is a musical in its own right. If you know the movie, you will find many of the familiar songs contained within these covers. But you will also find some other Irving Berlin songs that were added in order to make the adaptation valid as a Broadway musical on its own.

In 1954 Irving Berlin sketched out a plot of a new musical movie for Paramount Pictures to be called *White Christmas.* Its plot is pure post-World War II Hollywood: two successful song and dance men who met in the Army (Bob Wallace and Phil Davis) meet two singing sisters (Betty and Judy Haynes.) There are complications as they get to know one another, and finally they end up as two couples. The movie became a classic of its time, one of the few Hollywood musicals you could count on seeing on television each and every Christmas season.

The idea of turning *White Christmas* into a stage musical came into being around the turn of this century, when people at Paramount Pictures began conversations with Paul Blake, the artistic director of St. Louis' outdoor summer theater, affectionately called The Muny. Blake produced his own adaptation in 2000, which was attended by the three daughters of Irving Berlin, who ventured out to see whether there was a show. The answer was yes, and the road to Broadway began.

Enter Kevin McCollum, successful Broadway producer (*Rent, Avenue Q, The Drowsy Chaperone, In the Heights…*) who was once Blake's associate at the Muny. He brought in a team of Broadway pros including director Walter Bobbie, co-author David Ives, choreographer Randy Skinner, designers Anna Louizos (sets,) Carrie Robbins (costumes,) and Ken Billington (lights.) To give the score both a modern sensibility and yet a proper nod to the sound and feel of the musical movies of the 1950s, the music department was made up of dance and vocal arranger Bruce Pomahac, orchestrator Larry Blank and music director Rob Berman. McCollum's idea was to create a show that could be a holiday stage classic, performed across the country in cities that would share a production in alternating years. It was an innovative idea, and it worked.

And then in 2008, the opportunity arose to bring it to Broadway.

At the new stage musical's premiere engagement at San Francisco's Curran Theater, the *Oakland Tribune* wrote: "Step aside, *Christmas Carol*. Twirl back, *Nutcracker*. There's a new kid on the seasonal entertainment block and its star is Irving Berlin." And the *Contra Costa Times* said, "*White Christmas* is already a film classic, and it appears the stage version has a great shot at similar status."

Irving Berlin captured the essence of the Christmas holiday with the simple words: "I'm dreaming of a white Christmas." Who doesn't think about wintertime family gatherings, home and hearth, gift giving, and sharing—not to mention the longing to hold on to memories of past holidays—when we hear those words, set to the deceptively simple melody Irving Berlin wrote to go with them? His song first appeared in *Holiday Inn*, a 1942 confection of a film based on an idea of Berlin's to set a story in an inn that is only opened on the fifteen holidays of the year. (The well-known hotel chain actually got its moniker from the film.) Writing a number of holiday-related songs, Berlin was surprised when "White Christmas," sung by the film's star Bing Crosby, became the break-out hit. He had expected another song to take the honors, but the wistful song about Christmas not only became the most noted song of the score, but it won Berlin an Oscar®. In one song for one movie, Berlin had managed to take the focus away from a holiday steeped in Christian faith and put it squarely on the human, familial and emotional side of Christmas. To date, the Crosby version of the song has sold over 125 million records, making it the best-selling record in history.

The stage version of Irving Berlin's *White Christmas* has already delighted audiences across America, and across the ocean in the British Isles as well. Now it is a Broadway show. Whether you are experiencing these songs for the first time, or recalling memories from the past, this folio contains a remarkable collection of great Irving Berlin songs. They provide the score for the newest holiday classic musical. And it may be a cliché to say it, but they don't write them like this any more.

CONTENTS

HAPPY HOLIDAY

Words and Music by
IRVING BERLIN

Slowly

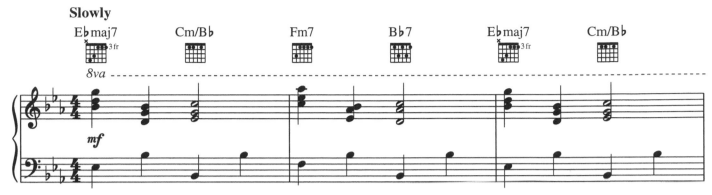

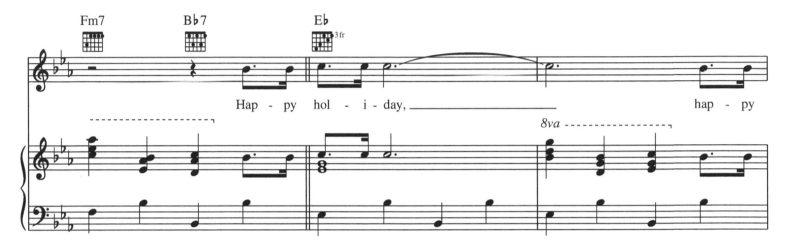

Hap - py hol - i - day, _____ hap - py

hol - i - day. _____ While the mer - ry bells keep

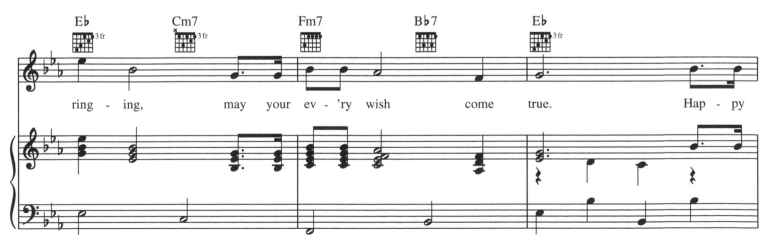

ring - ing, may your ev - 'ry wish come true. Hap - py

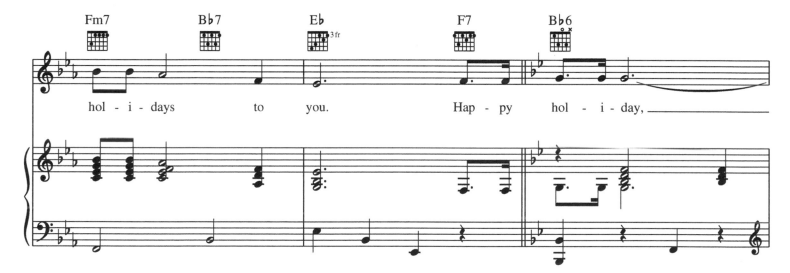

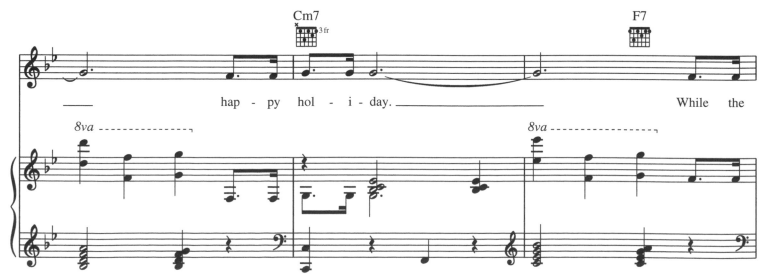

LET YOURSELF GO

Words and Music by
IRVING BERLIN

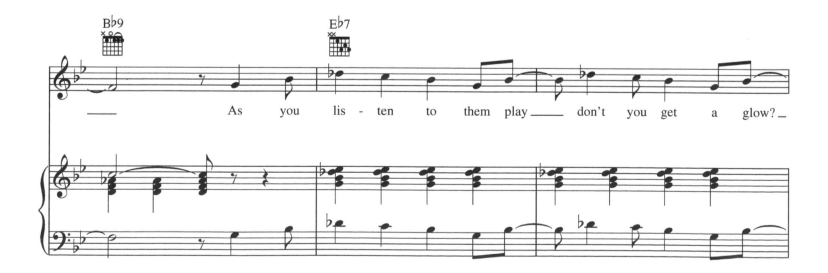

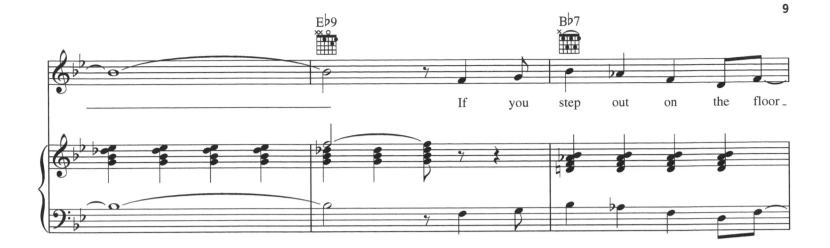

If you step out on the floor

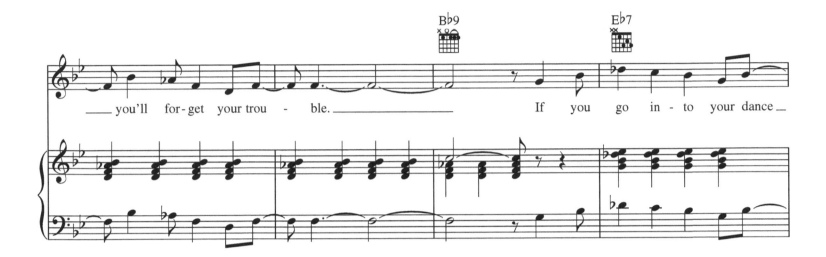

you'll for-get your trou - ble. If you go in - to your dance

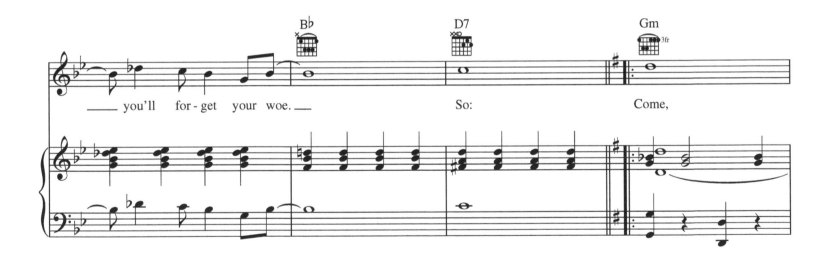

you'll for-get your woe. So: Come,

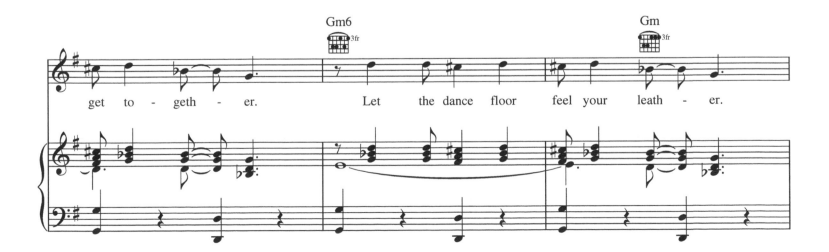

get to - geth - er. Let the dance floor feel your leath - er.

10

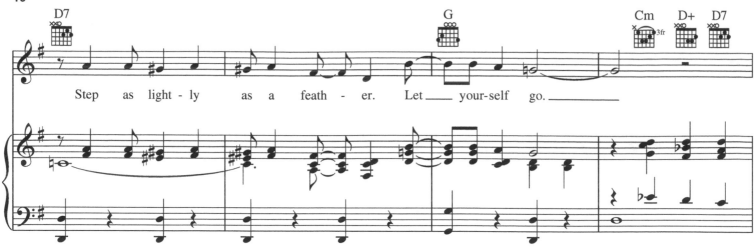

Step as light-ly as a feath - er. Let ___ your-self go. ___

Come hit the tim - ber. Loos - en up and start to lim - ber.

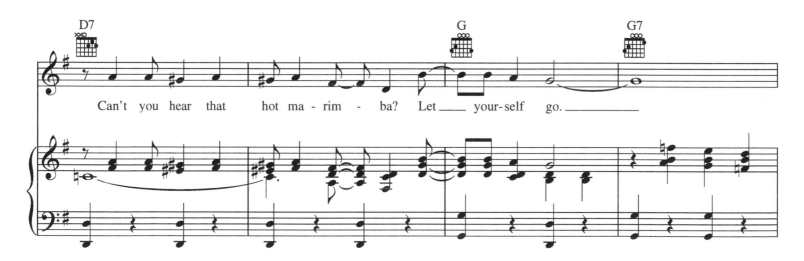

Can't you hear that hot ma - rim - ba? Let ___ your-self go. ___

Let your-self go, ___ re - lax, and let your-self go. ___ Re-lax, you've

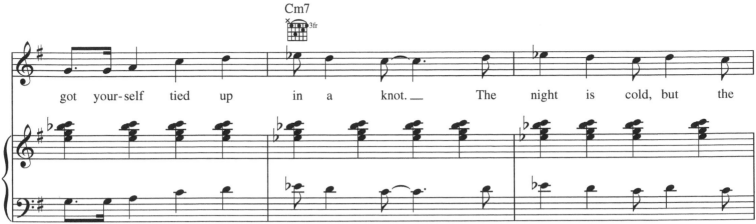

Cm7

got your-self tied up in a knot. ___ The night is cold, but the

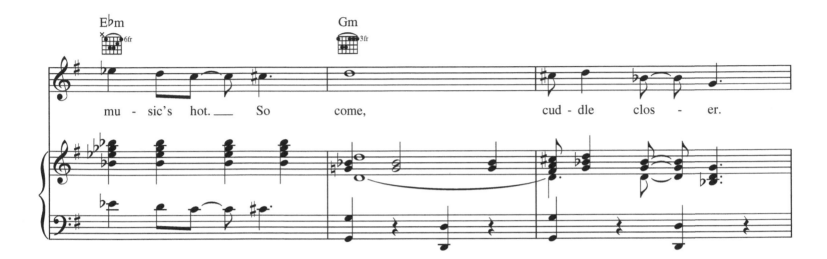

Ebm   Gm

mu - sic's hot. ___ So come,   cud - dle clos - er.

Gm6   Gm   D7

Don't you dare to an - swer, "No ___ sir."   Butch - er, bank - er,

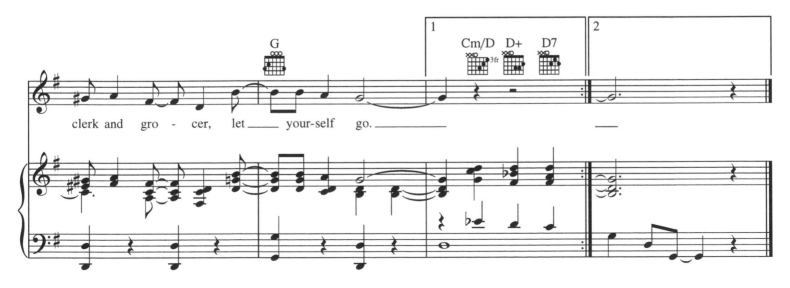

G   1   Cm/D   D+   D7   2

clerk and gro - cer, let ___ your-self go. ___

LOVE AND THE WEATHER

Words and Music by
IRVING BERLIN

SISTERS

Words and Music by
IRVING BERLIN

Moderately

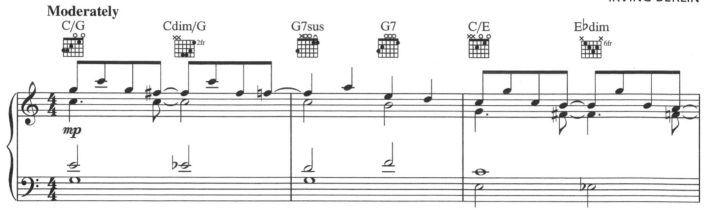

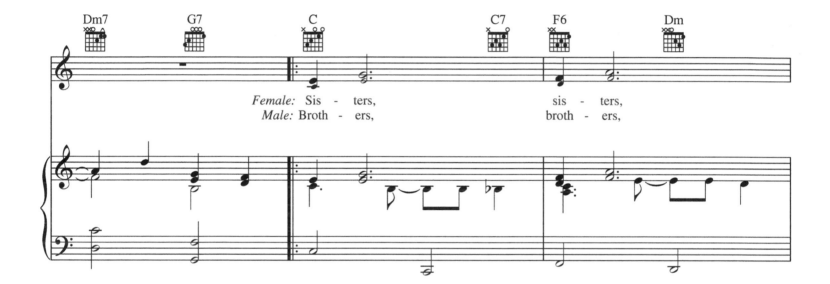

Female: Sis - ters,
Male: Broth - ers,

sis - ters,
broth - ers,

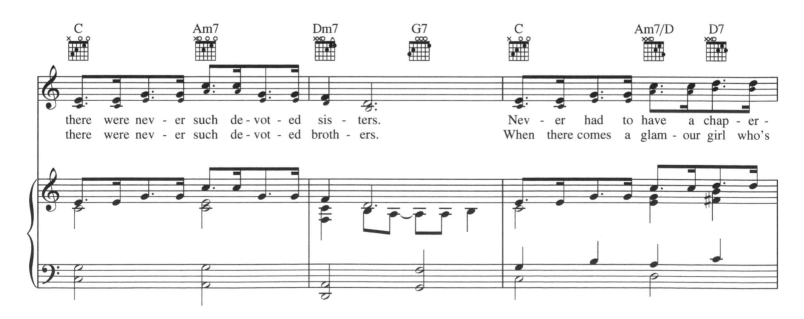

there were nev - er such de - vot - ed sis - ters.
there were nev - er such de - vot - ed broth - ers.

Nev - er had to have a chap - er -
When there comes a glam - our girl who's

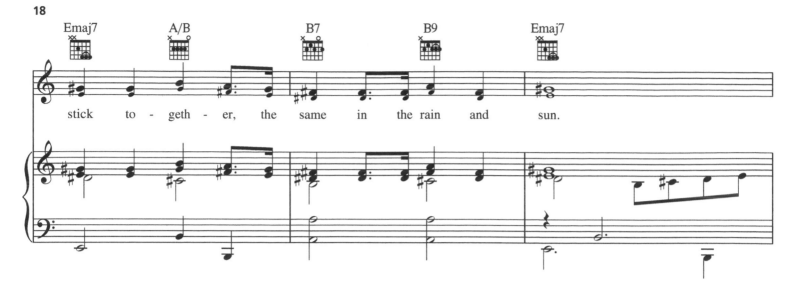

stick to - geth - er, the same in the rain and sun.

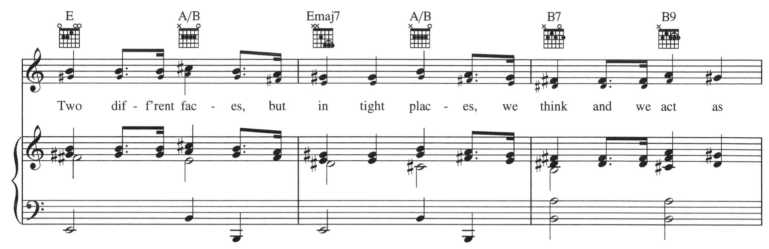

Two dif - f'rent fac - es, but in tight plac - es, we think and we act as

one. _____ Those who've seen us

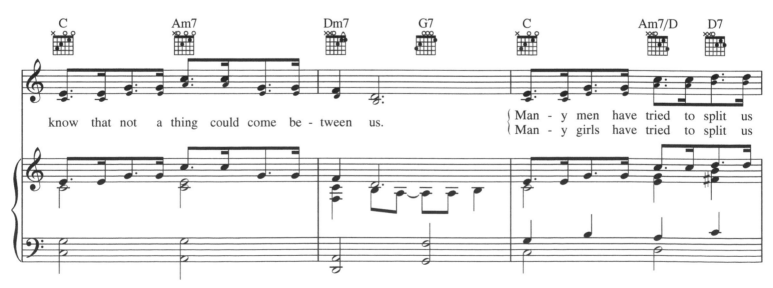

know that not a thing could come be - tween us.

Man - y men have tried to split us
Man - y girls have tried to split us

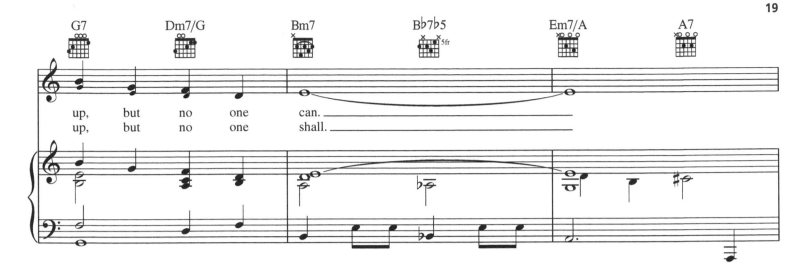

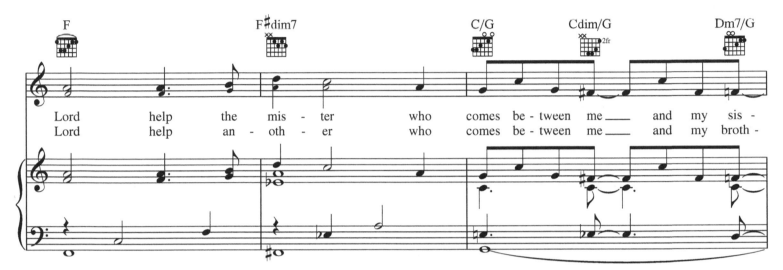

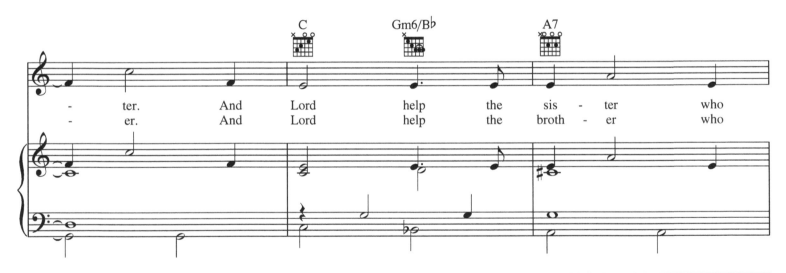

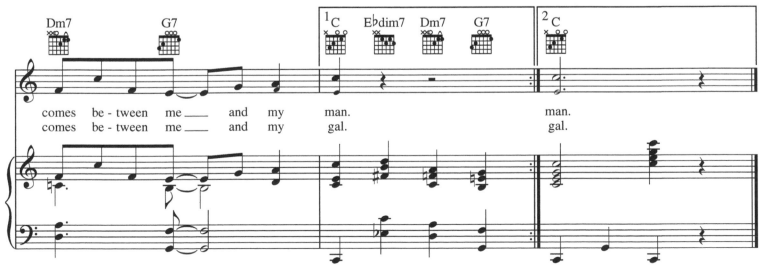

THE BEST THINGS HAPPEN WHILE YOU'RE DANCING

Words and Music by
IRVING BERLIN

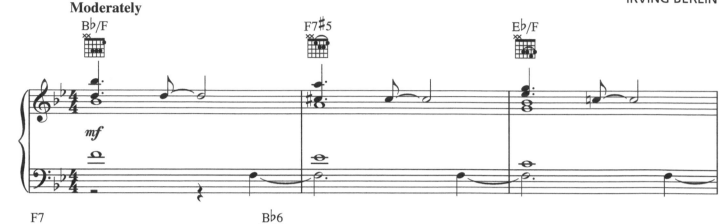

The best things _____ hap-pen while you're danc - ing; _____ Things that you would not do at home Come

nat - ur - 'lly on the floor. _____ For

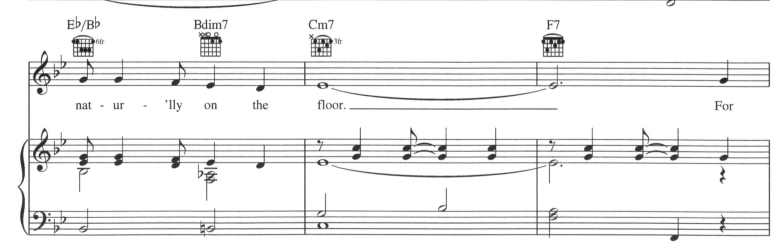

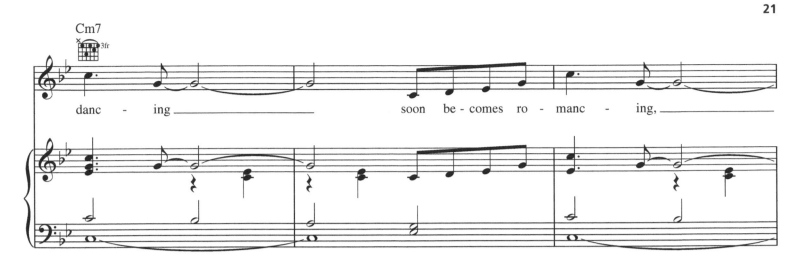

danc - ing _____ soon be - comes ro - manc - ing, _____

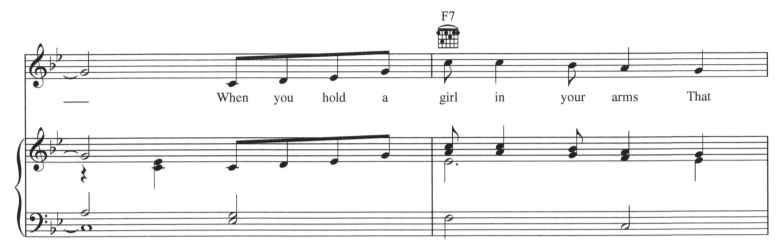

____ When you hold a girl in your arms That

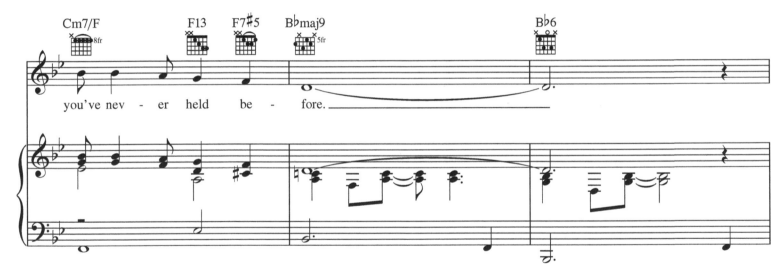

you've nev - er held be - fore. _____

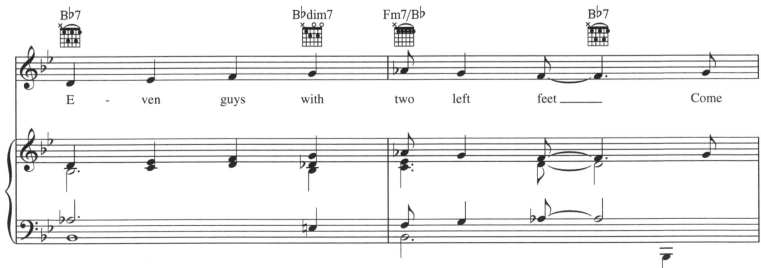

E - ven guys with two left feet ____ Come

SNOW

Words and Music by
IRVING BERLIN

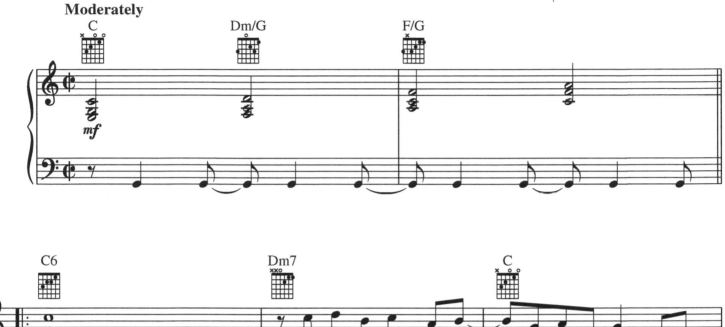

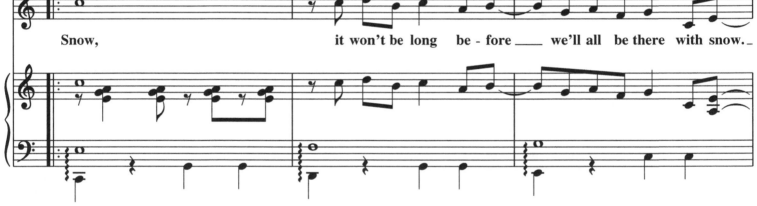

Snow,   it won't be long be - fore ____ we'll all be there with snow. ___

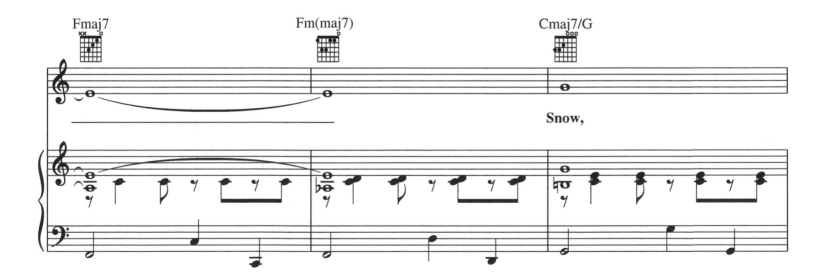

Snow,

WHAT CAN YOU DO WITH A GENERAL

Words and Music by
IRVING BERLIN

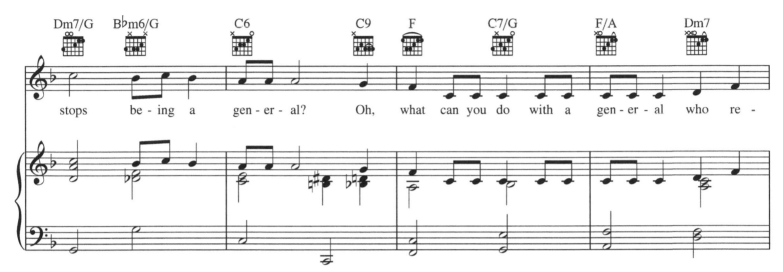

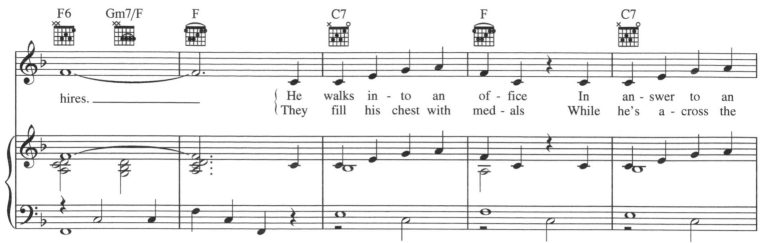

hires. _____

He walks in-to an of-fice In an-swer to an
They fill his chest with med-als While he's a-cross the

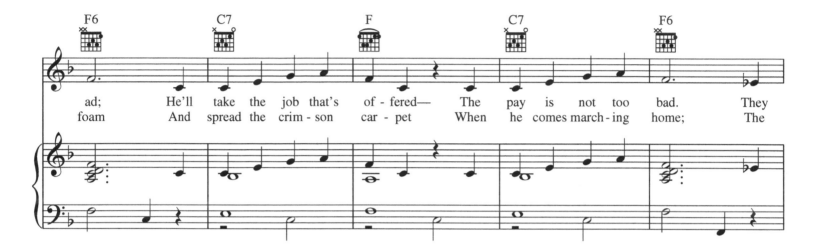

ad; He'll take the job that's of-fered— The pay is not too bad. They
foam And spread the crim-son car-pet When he comes march-ing home; The

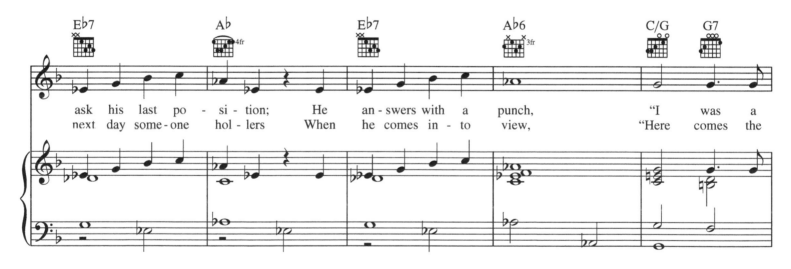

ask his last po - si - tion; He an-swers with a punch, "I was a
next day some-one hol-lers When he comes in - to view, "Here comes the

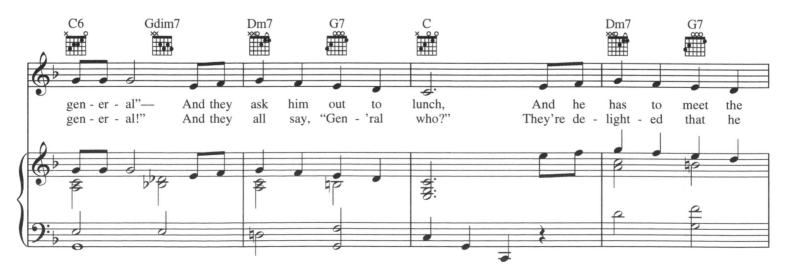

gen - er - al"— And they ask him out to lunch, And he has to meet the
gen - er - al!" And they all say, "Gen - 'ral who?" They're de-light-ed that he

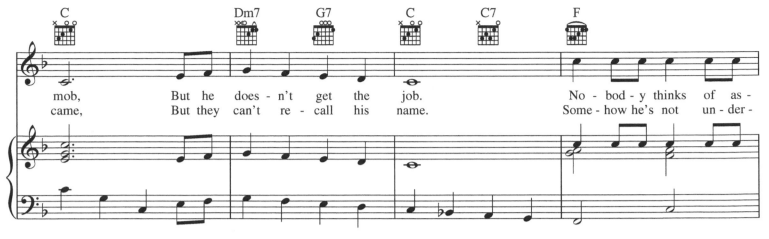

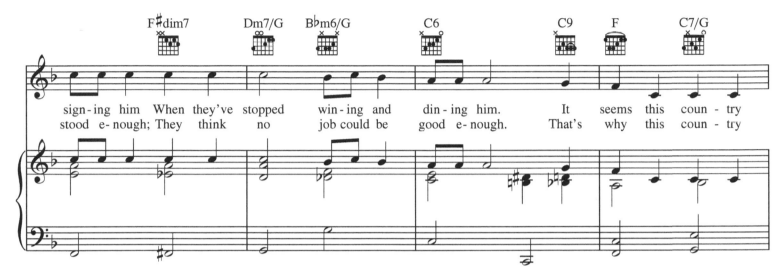

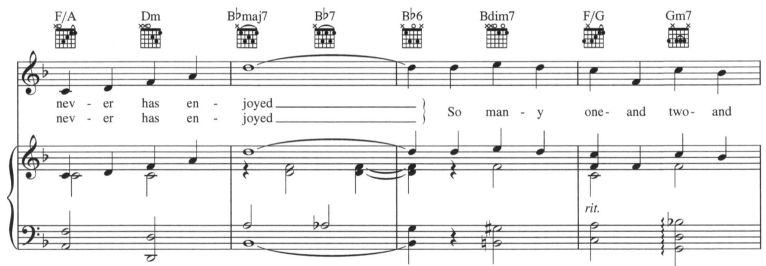

LET ME SING AND I'M HAPPY

Words and Music by
IRVING BERLIN

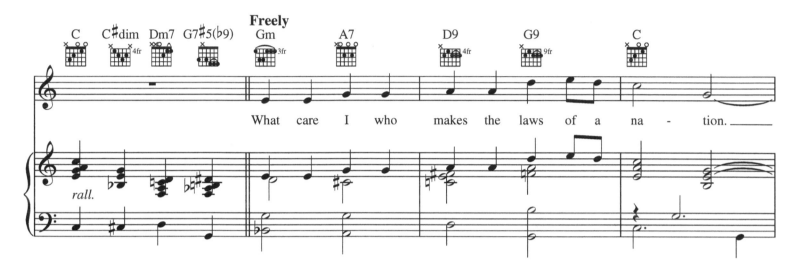

What care I who makes the laws of a na - tion. _____

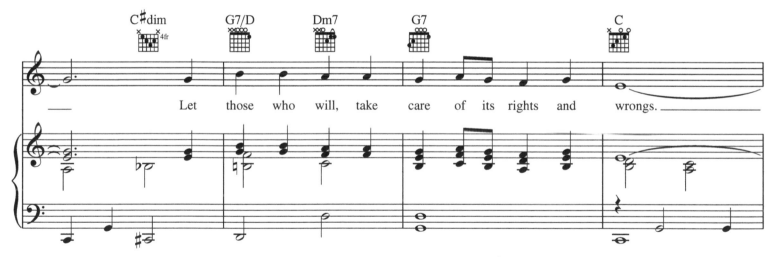

_____ Let those who will, take care of its rights and wrongs. _____

_____ What care I who cares for the world's af -

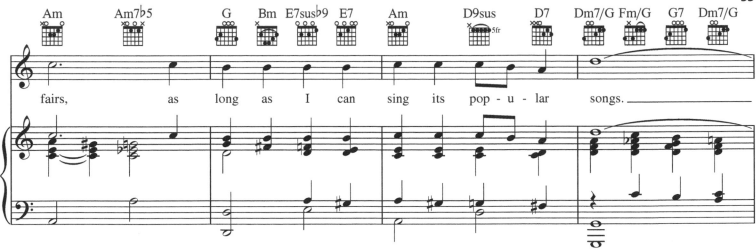

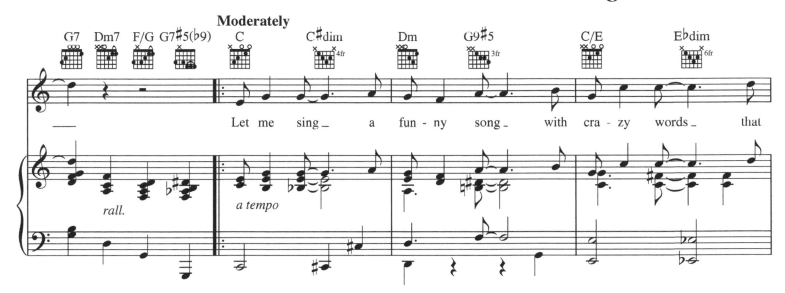

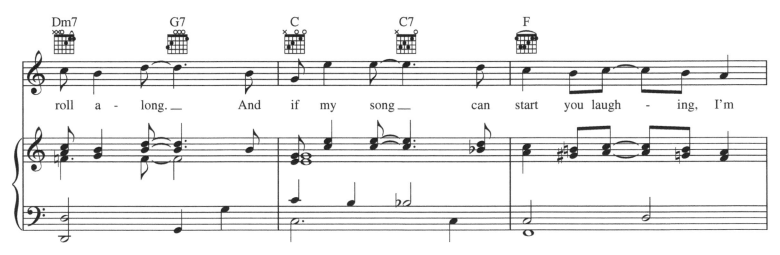

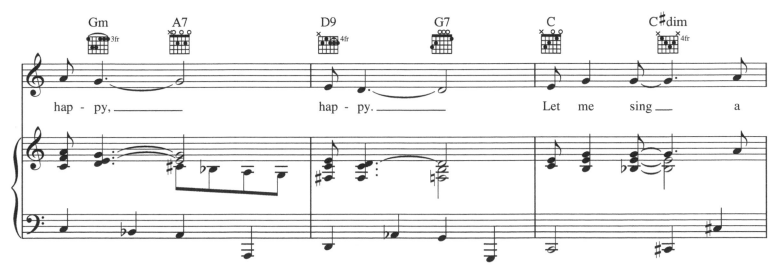

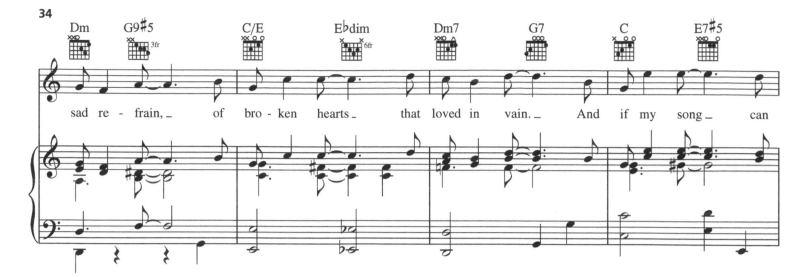

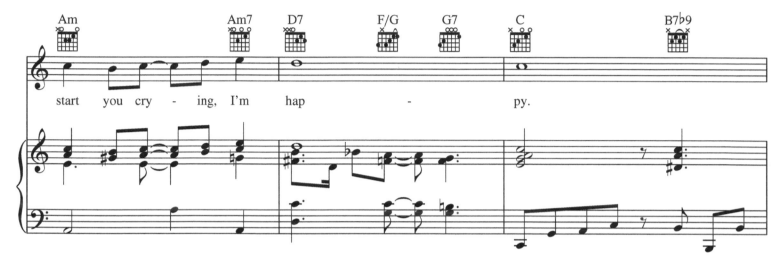

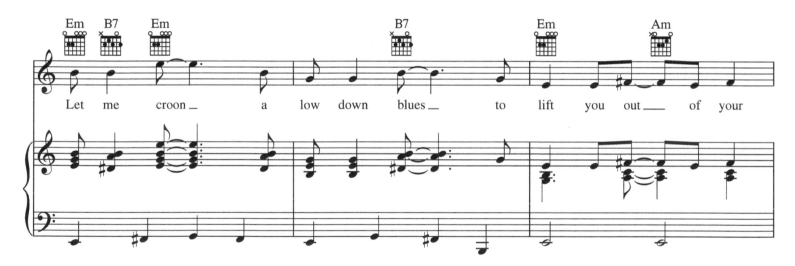

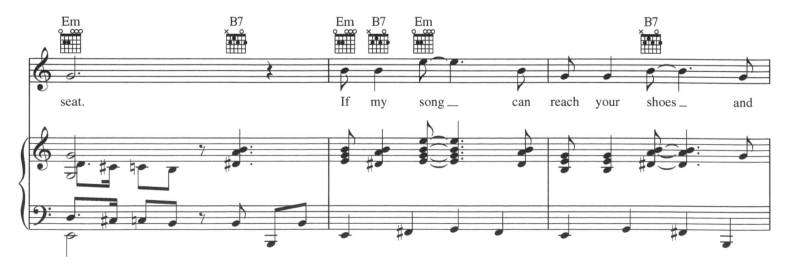

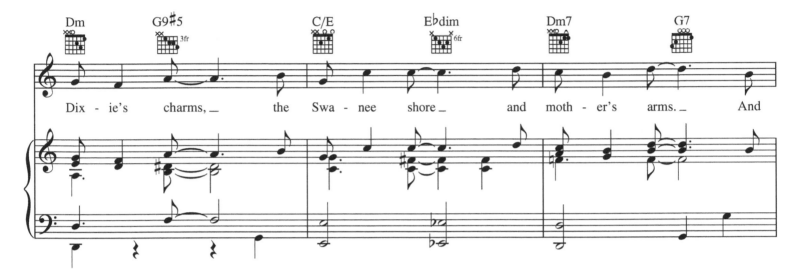

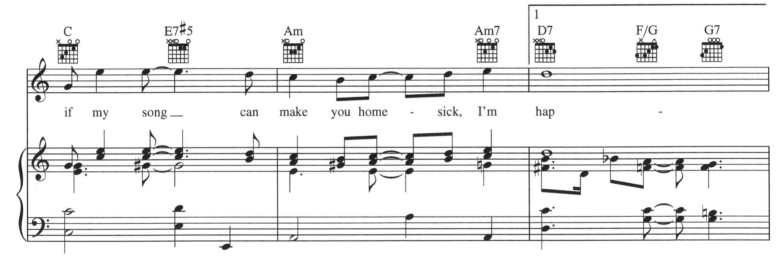

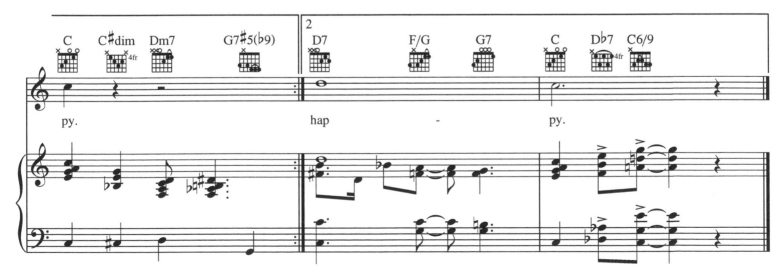

The Berlin Family, Christmas, 1942. Elizabeth, Irving, Mary Ellin, wife Ellin, and Linda.
Photo courtesy of the Irving Berlin Estate.

COUNT YOUR BLESSINGS INSTEAD OF SHEEP

Words and Music by
IRVING BERLIN

get - ting small, __ I think of when I had none at all. __ And

I fall a - sleep __ count - ing my bless -

ings. I think a - bout a nurs - 'ry and __ I

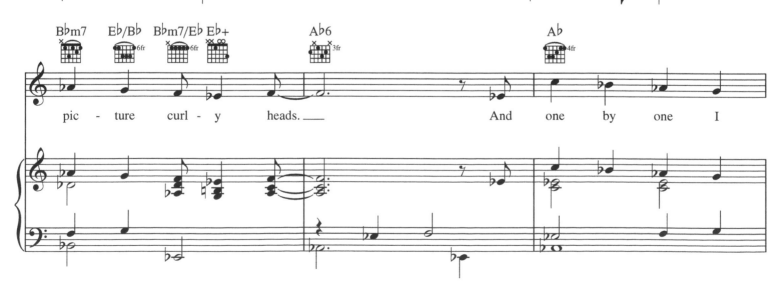

pic - ture curl - y heads. __ And one by one I

BLUE SKIES

Words and Music by
IRVING BERLIN

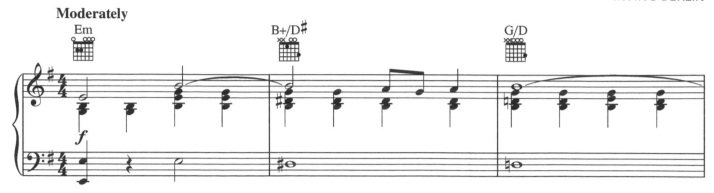

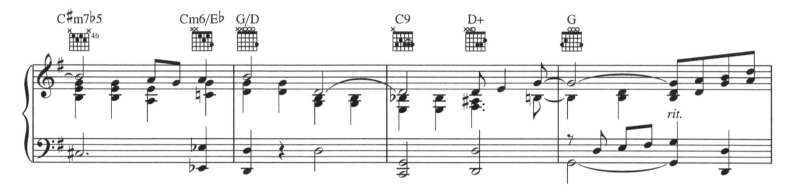

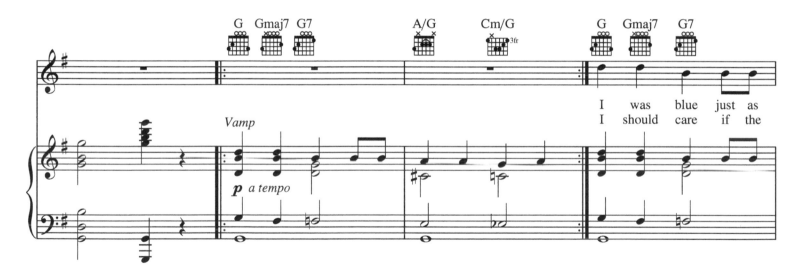

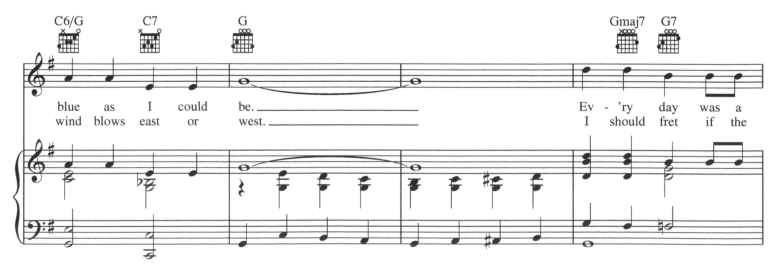

I was blue just as
I should care if the

blue as I could be. _____
wind blows east or west. _____

Ev - 'ry day was a
I should fret if the

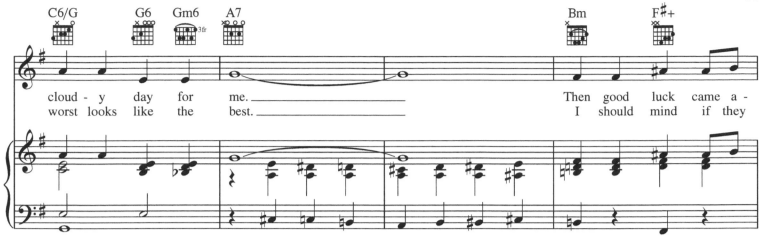

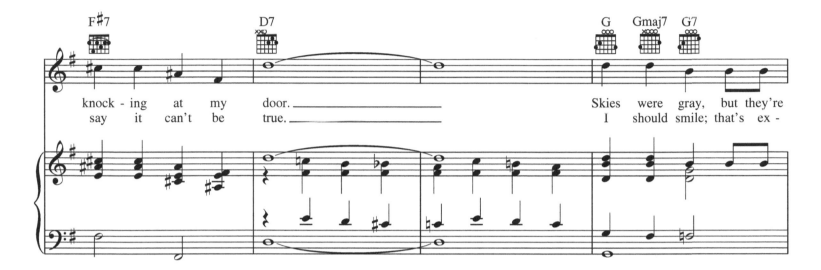

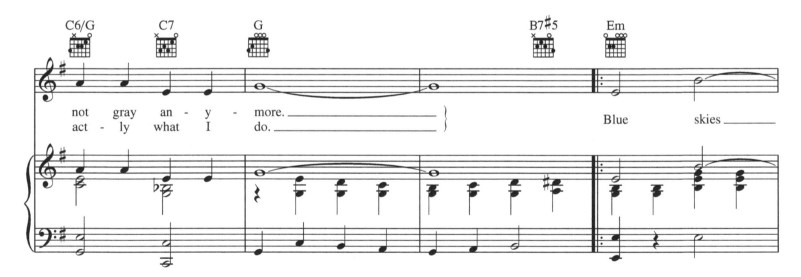

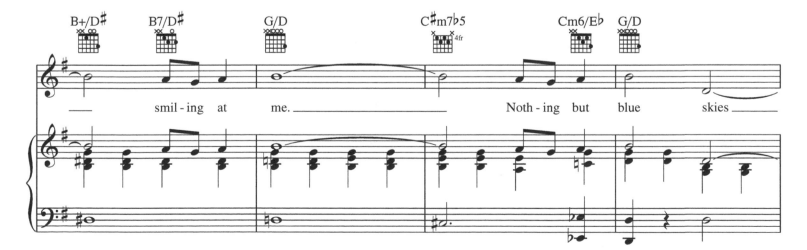

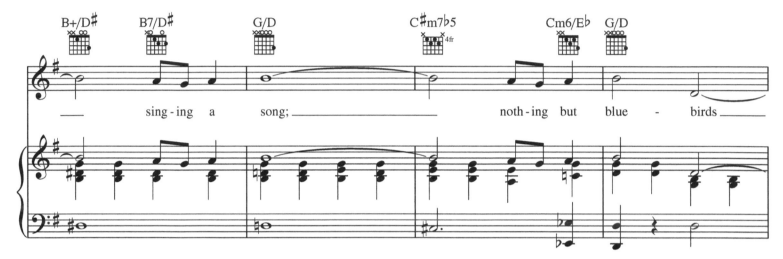

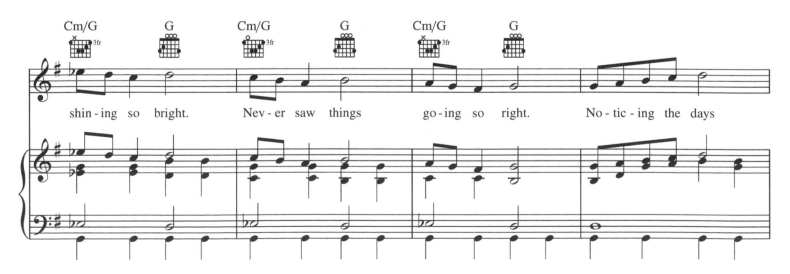

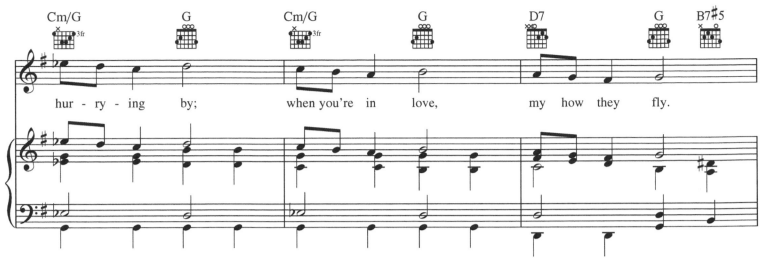

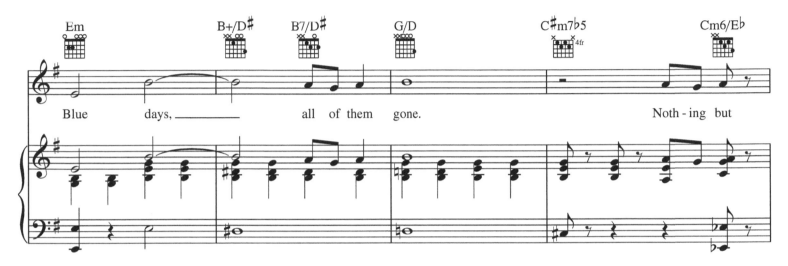

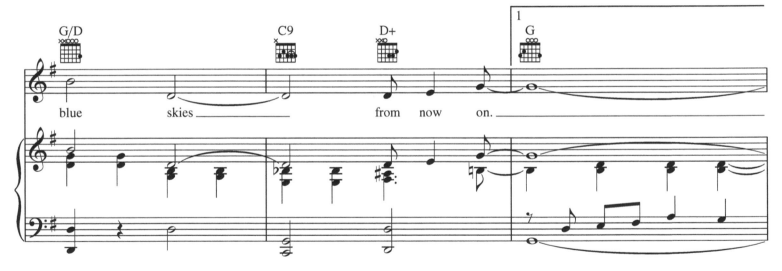

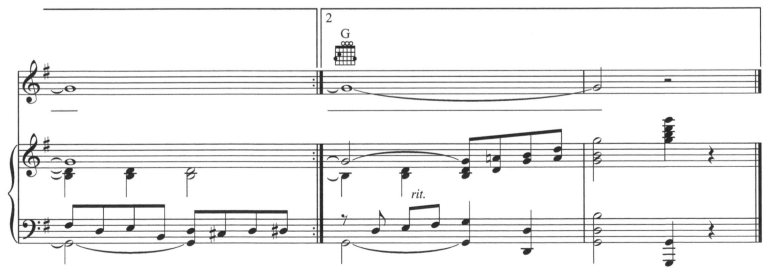

I LOVE A PIANO

Words and Music by
IRVING BERLIN

As a child, I went wild when a band played. How I
When a green Tet - ra - zine starts to war - ble, I grow

ran to the man when his hand swayed. Clar - i - nets were my pets, and a
cold as an old piece of mar - ble. I al - lude to the crude lit - tle

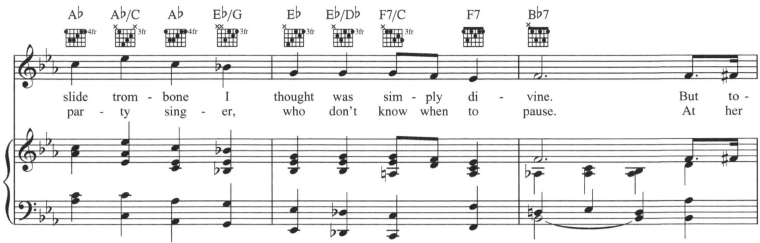

slide trom - bone I thought was sim - ply di - vine. But to - her
par - ty sing - er, who don't know when to pause. At her

day, when they play, I could hiss them. Ev - 'ry bar is a jar to my
best I de - test the so - pran - o, but I run to the one at the

sys - tem. But there's one mu - si - cal in - stru - ment, that
pian - o. I al - ways love the ac - comp - 'ni - ment and

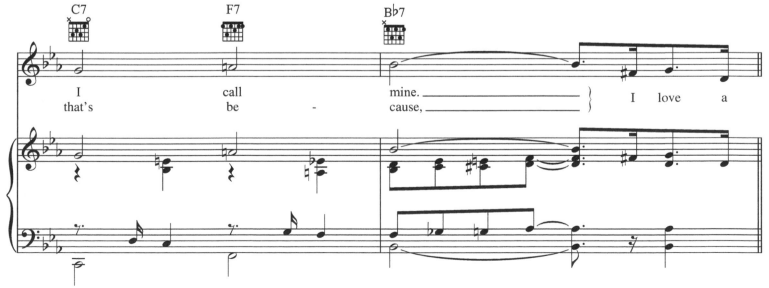

I call mine. I love a
that's be - cause, I love a

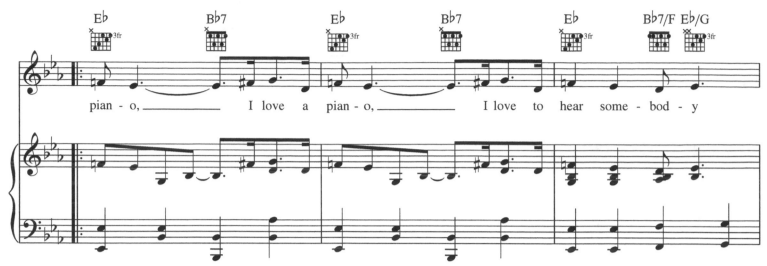

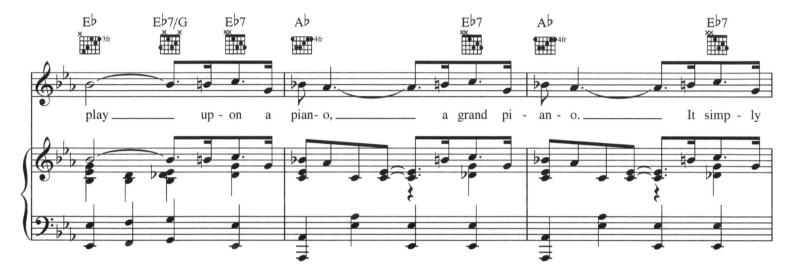

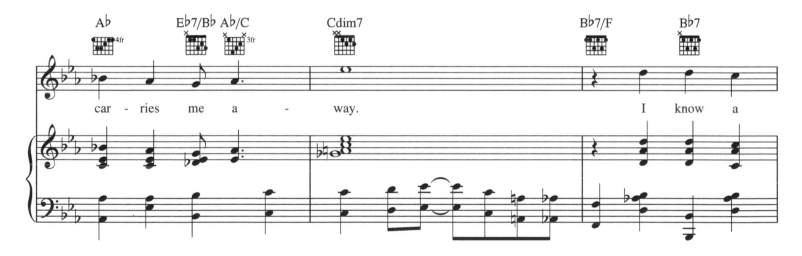

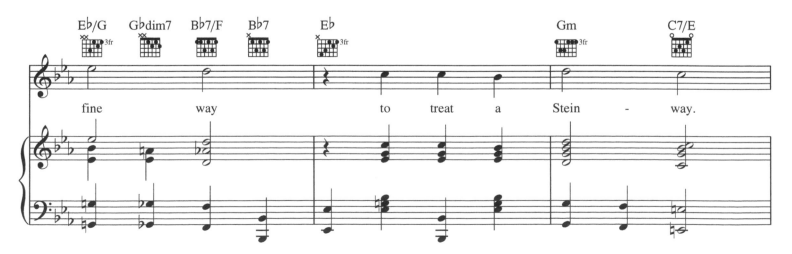

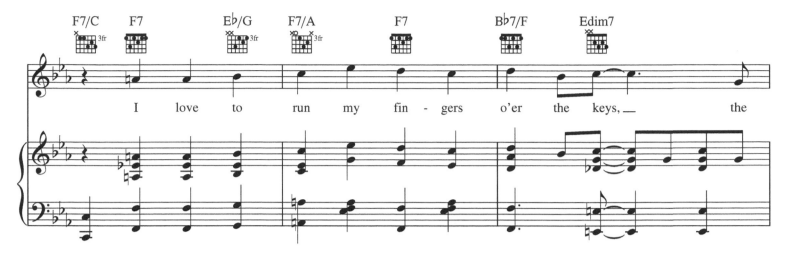

I love to run my fin - gers o'er the keys, the

i - vo - ries. And with the ped - al I love to

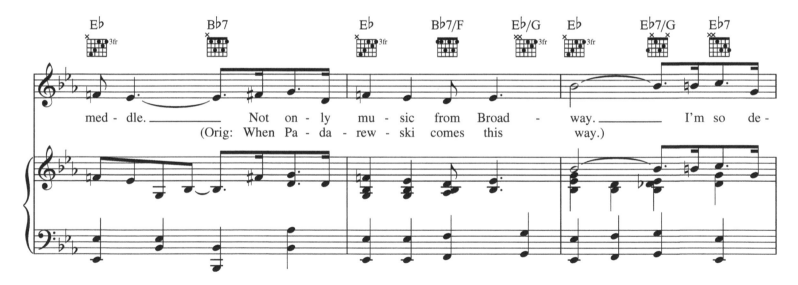

med - dle. Not on - ly mu - sic from Broad - way. I'm so de -
(Orig: When Pa - da - rew - ski comes this way.)

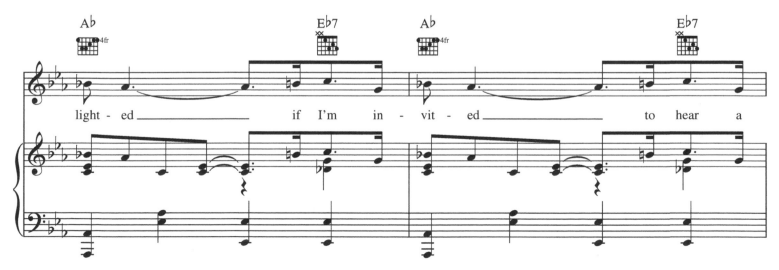

light - ed if I'm in - vit - ed to hear a

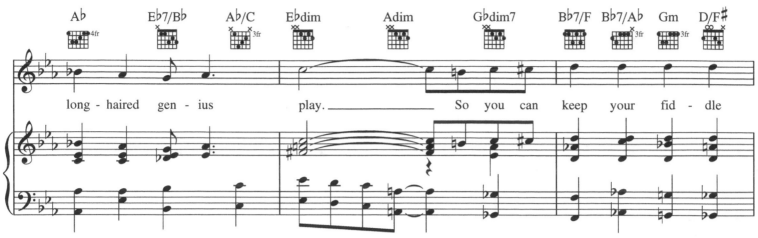

long - haired gen - ius play. _____ So you can keep your fid - dle

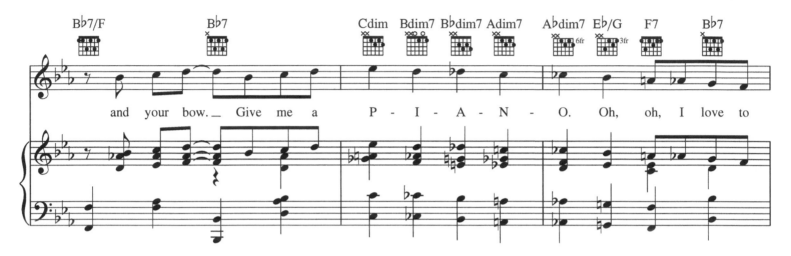

and your bow._ Give me a P - I - A - N - O. Oh, oh, I love to

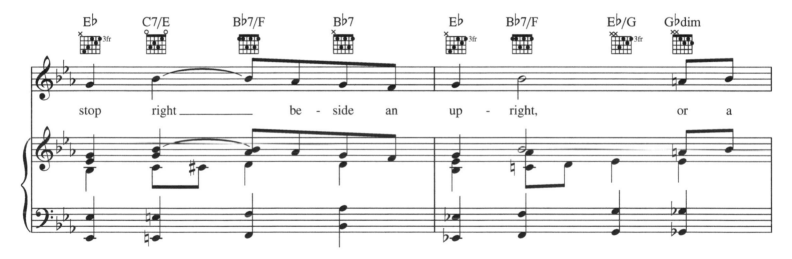

stop right _____ be - side an up - right, or a

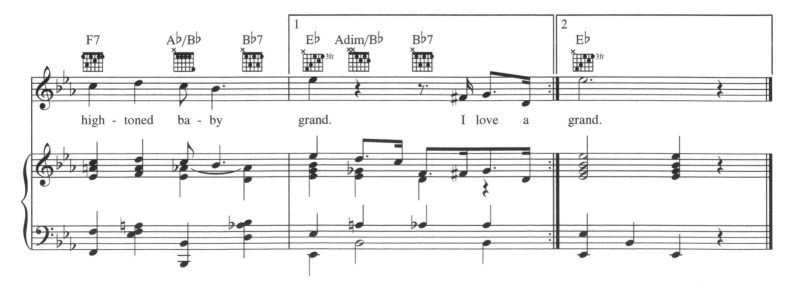

high - toned ba - by grand. I love a grand.

FALLING OUT OF LOVE CAN BE FUN

Words and Music by
IRVING BERLIN

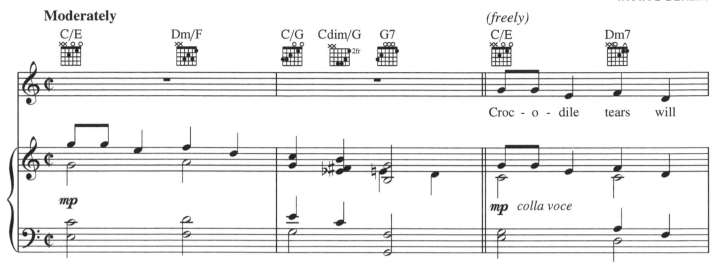

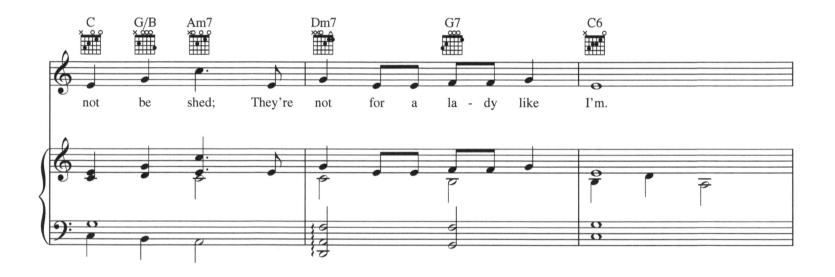

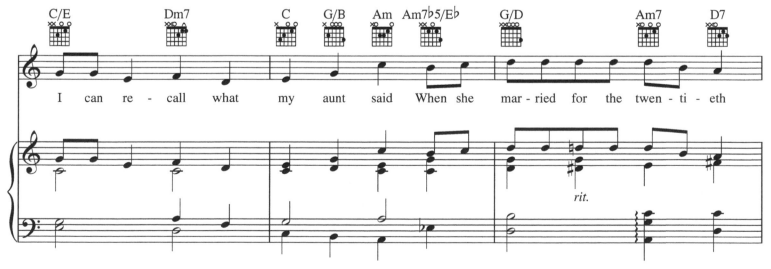

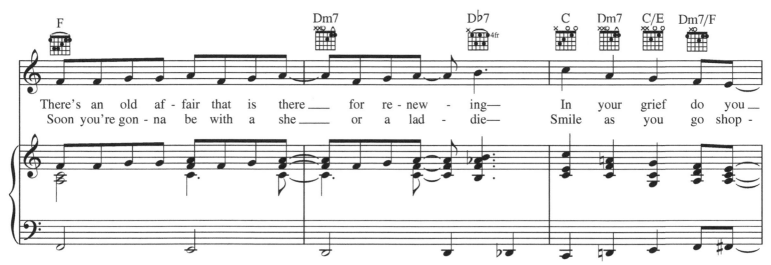

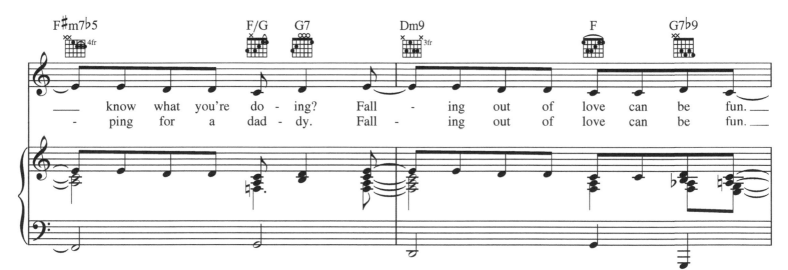

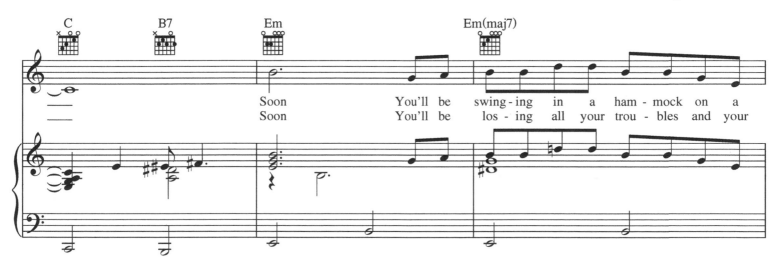

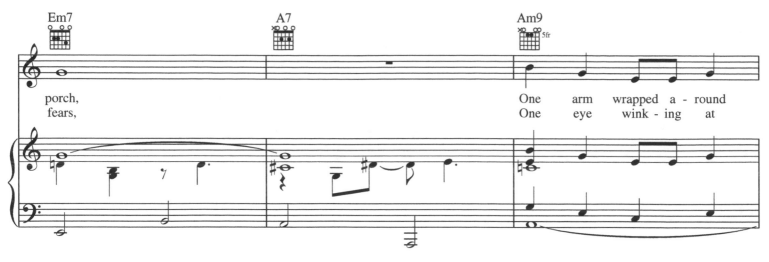

porch,
fears,

One arm wrapped a - round
One eye wink - ing at

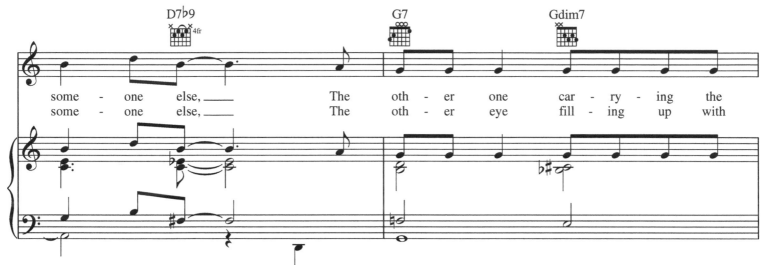

some - one else, _____ The oth - er one car - ry - ing the
some - one else, _____ The oth - er eye fill - ing up with

torch.
tears.

Love can give a la - dy a clout, _____
When you find your lov - ing ro - mance _____

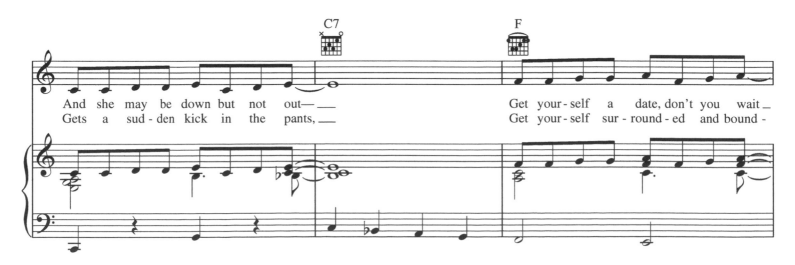

And she may be down but not out— _____
Gets a sud - den kick in the pants, _____

Get your - self a date, don't you wait _
Get your - self sur - round - ed and bound -

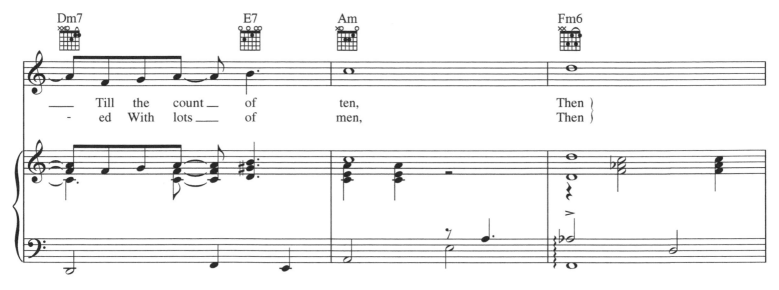

Till the count ___ of ten,
-ed With lots ___ of men,
Then
Then

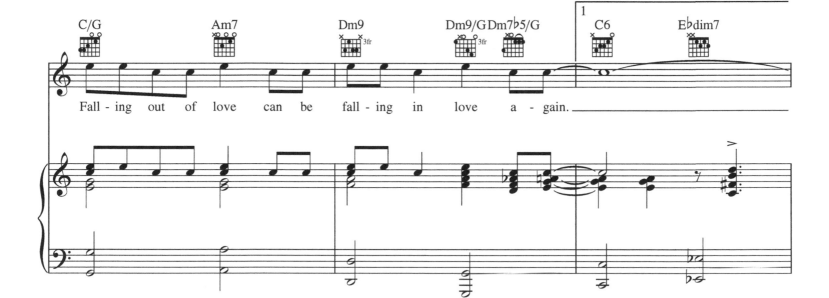

Fall-ing out of love can be fall-ing in love a-gain. ___

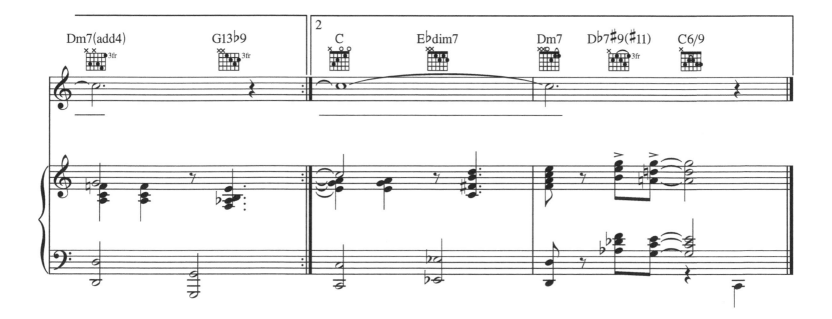

LOVE, YOU DIDN'T DO RIGHT BY ME

Words and Music by
IRVING BERLIN

HOW DEEP IS THE OCEAN
(How High Is the Sky)

Words and Music by
IRVING BERLIN

Moderately

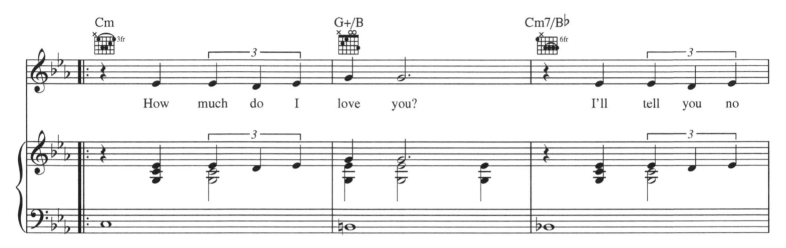

How much do I love you? I'll tell you no

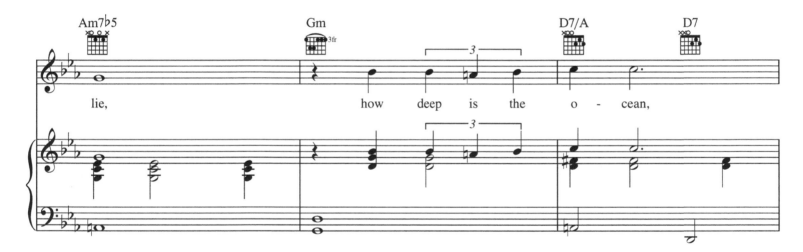

lie, how deep is the o - cean,

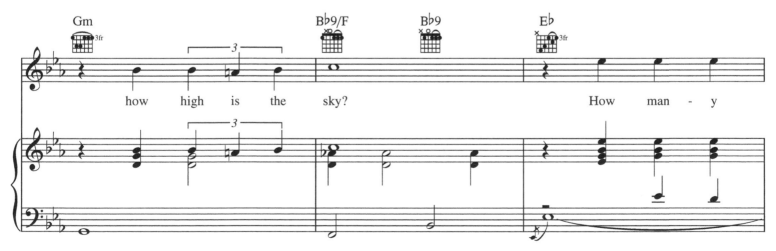

how high is the sky? How man - y

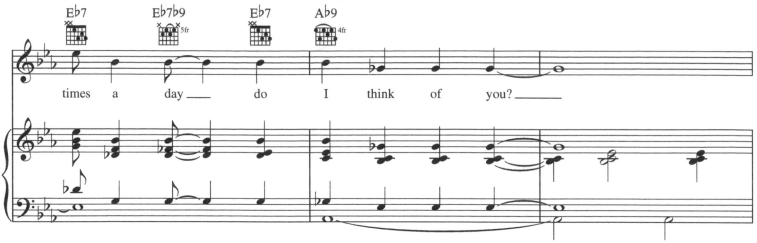

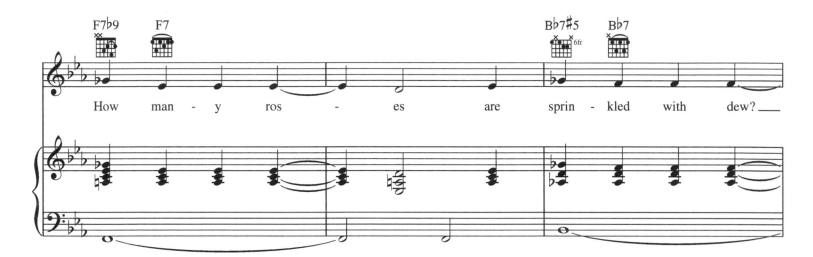

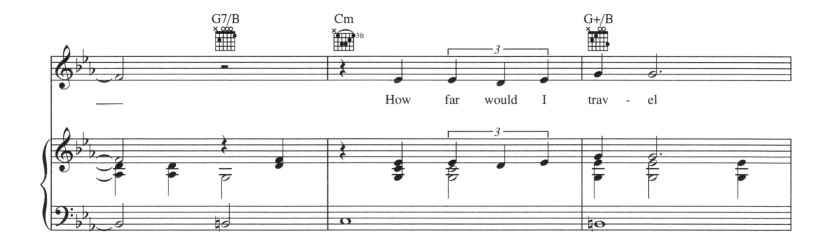

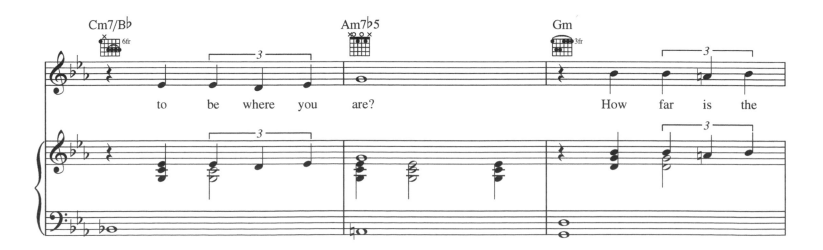

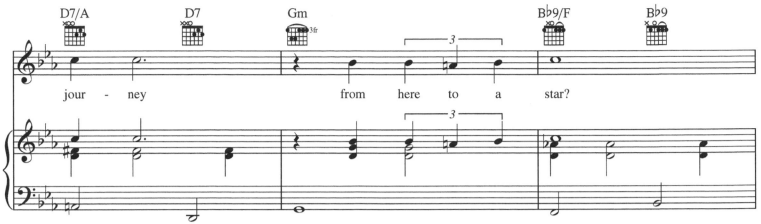

jour - ney   from   here   to   a   star?

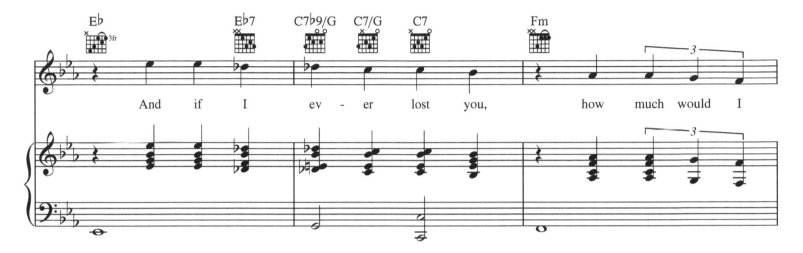

And   if   I   ev - er   lost   you,   how   much   would   I

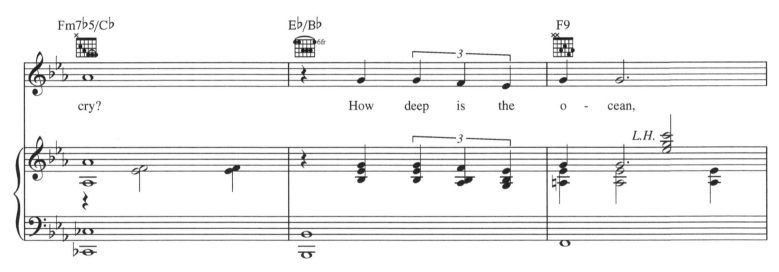

cry?   How   deep   is   the   o - cean,

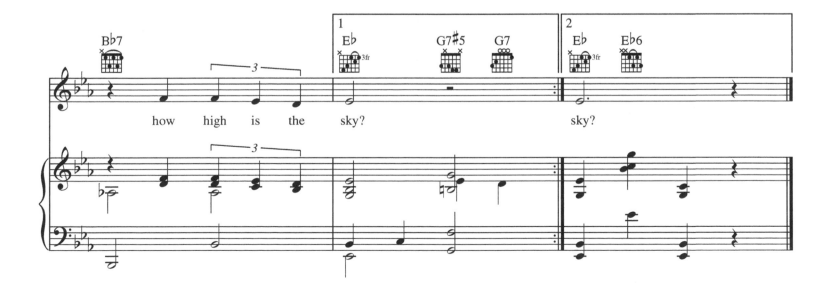

how   high   is   the   sky?   sky?

THE OLD MAN

Words and Music by
IRVING BERLIN

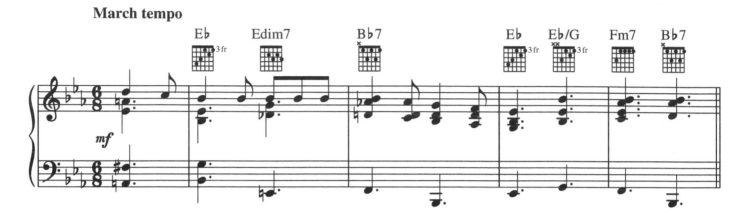

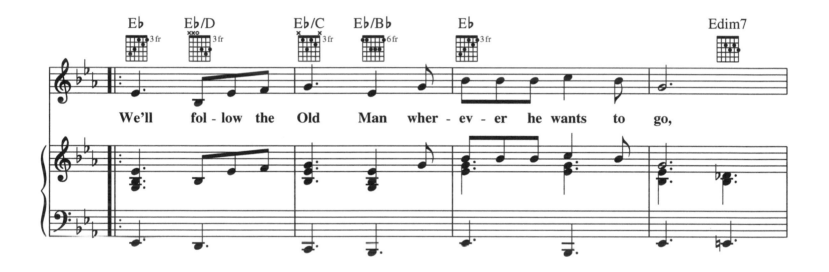

We'll fol-low the Old Man wher-ev-er he wants to go,

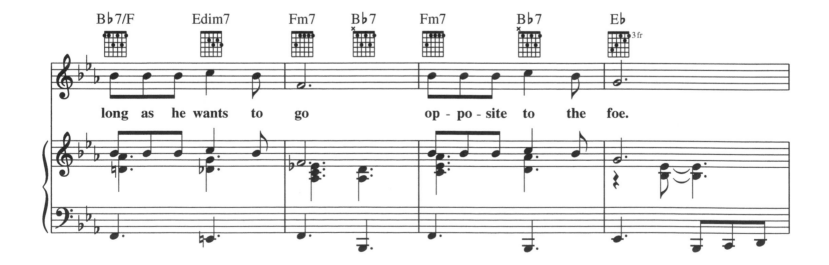

long as he wants to go op-po-site to the foe.

WHITE CHRISTMAS

Words and Music by
IRVING BERLIN

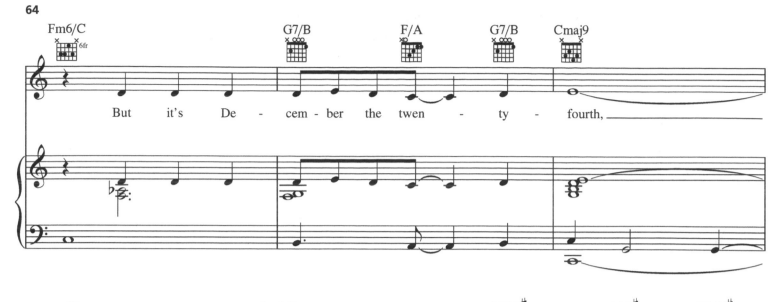

But it's De - cem - ber the twen - ty - fourth, _____

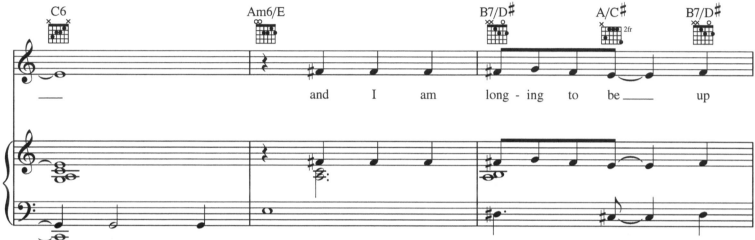

_____ and I am long - ing to be ____ up

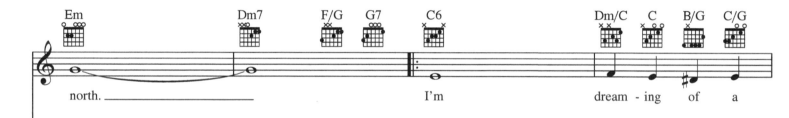

north. _____ I'm dream - ing of a

white Christ - mas, just like the

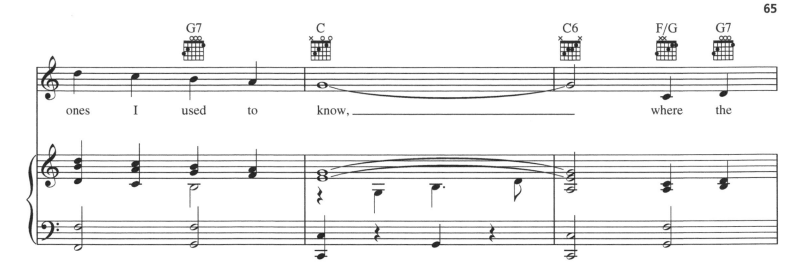
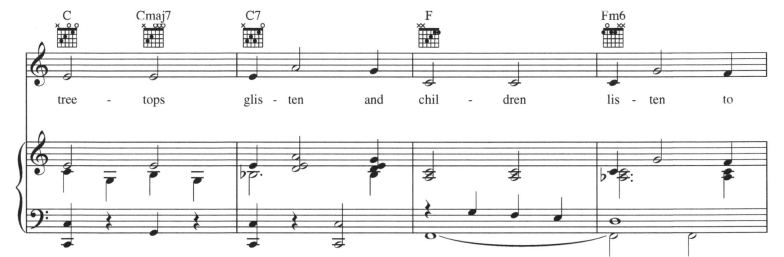
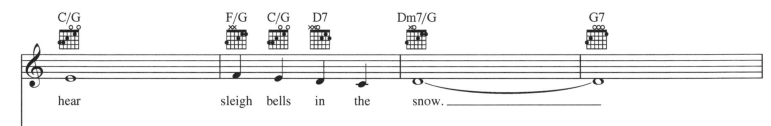
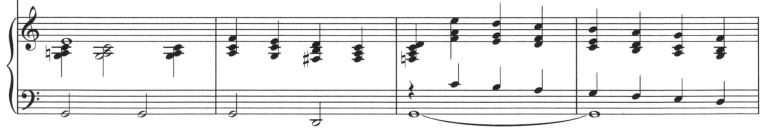
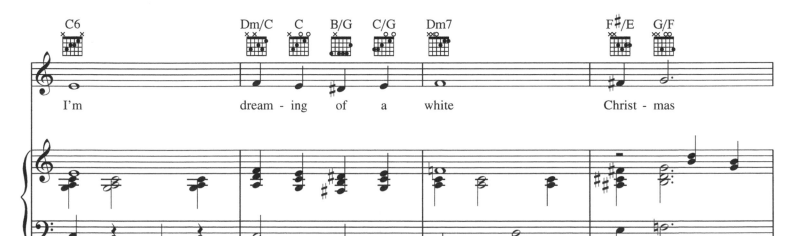

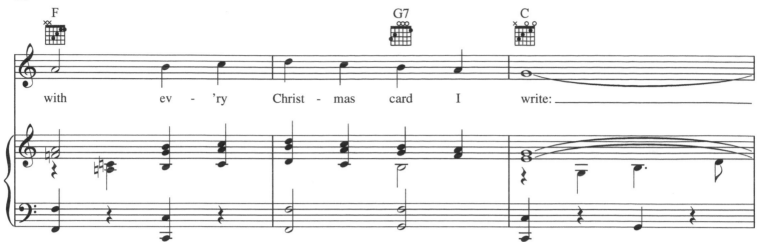

with ev - 'ry Christ - mas card I write:____

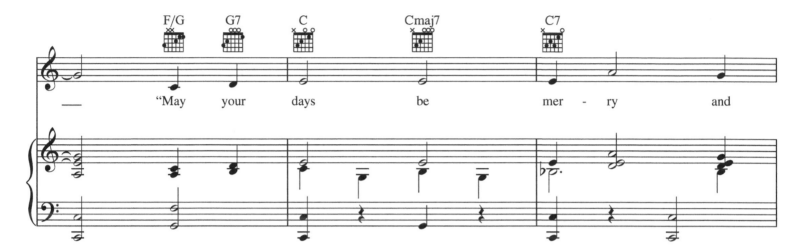

____ "May your days be mer - ry and

bright _____ and may all your Christ - mas - es be

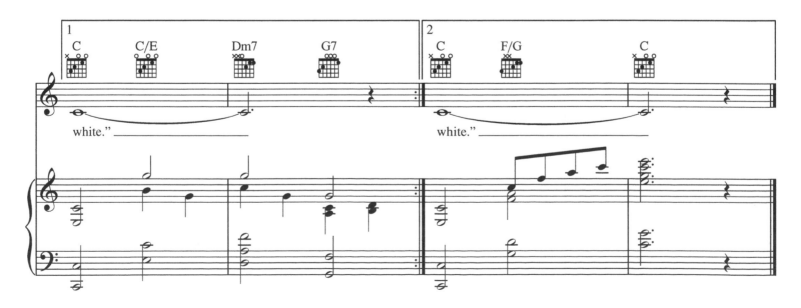

white."_____   white."_____

White Christmas

by
Irving Berlin

IRVING BERLIN Inc.
Music Publishers
799 SEVENTH AVE., NEW YORK, N.Y.

Early sheet music cover. One of Irving Berlin's biggest hits, "White Christmas" was actually introduced in the film HOLIDAY INN and was the winner of the 1942 Academy Award® for Best Original Song. Bing Crosby's recording is the best-selling record in history.

I'VE GOT MY LOVE TO KEEP ME WARM

Words and Music by
IRVING BERLIN

Bright Jump tempo

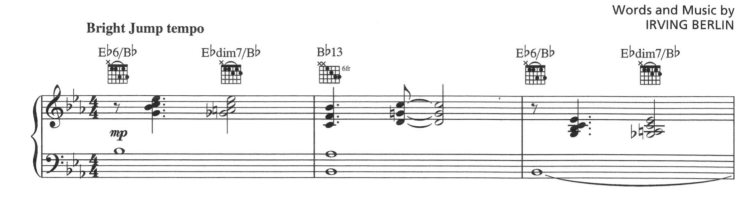

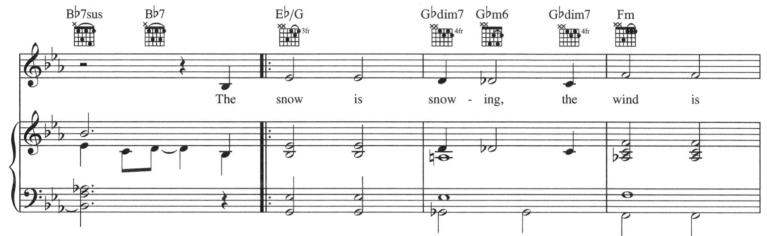

The snow is snow-ing, the wind is

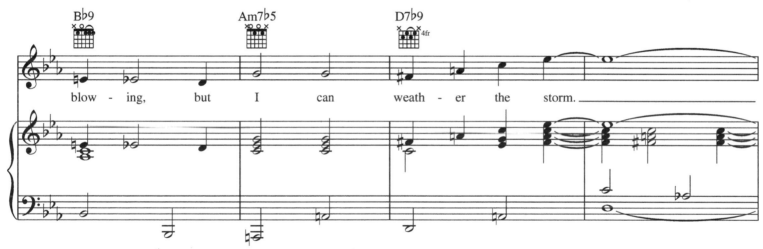

blow-ing, but I can weath-er the storm.

What do I care how much it may storm?

I've got my love to keep me warm.

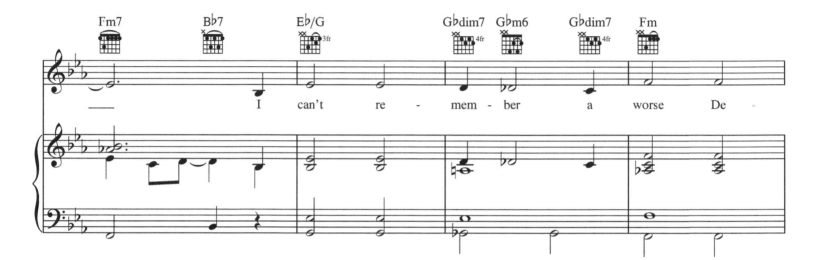

I can't re - mem - ber a worse De

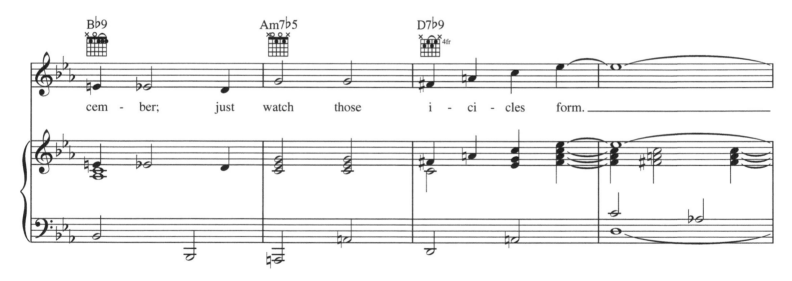

cem - ber; just watch those i - ci - cles form.

What do I care if i - ci - cles form?

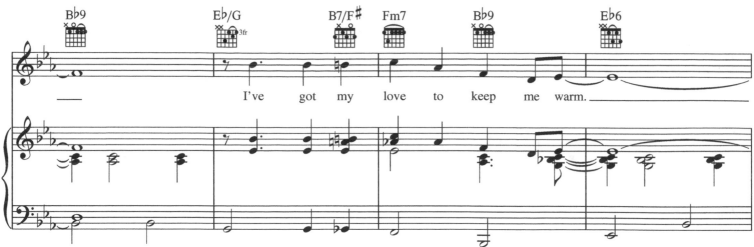

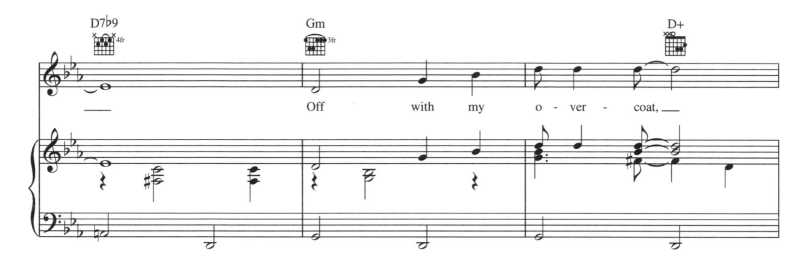

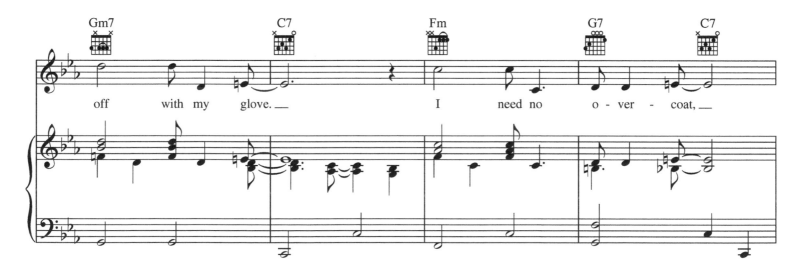

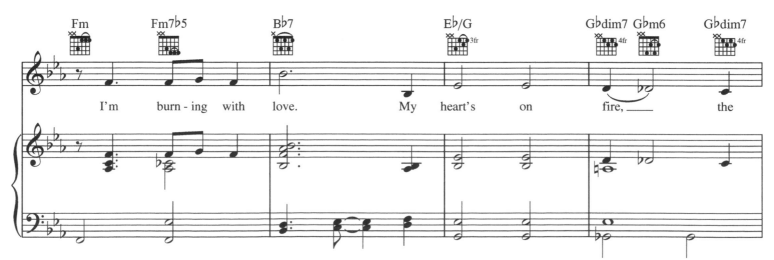

flame grows high - er, so I will weath - er the storm.

What do I care how much it may storm? __

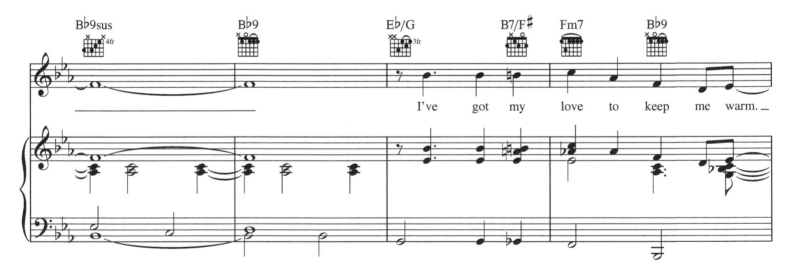

I've got my love to keep me warm. __

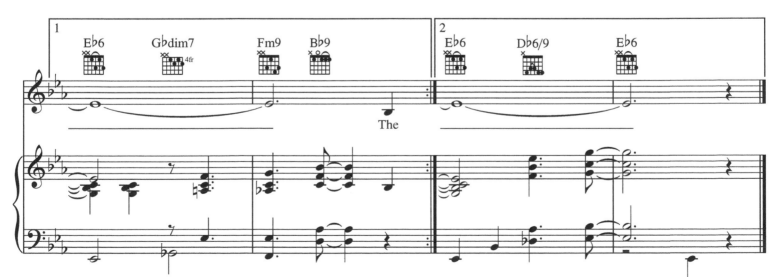

The